At last! A self-help book directed to th **and growing concerns of the Gay male! Gregor** **` written a sharp-eyed (and -tongued) and happ** **` Gay Life in this gossipy, profoundly lovin** **nd highly controversial new work. Floo** **many of the "cherished misconception** **.ch Gays and Straights both harbor--and i.** **ɔ, directed almost entirely to people who have** **re far removed from the usual "Be brave, draw up y** **.ıd die graciously."**

BROB HOUSE BOOKS
Atlanta

I'm Looking for
Mr. Right
but I'll Settle for
Mr. Right Away

I'm Looking for Mr. Right but I'll Settle for Mr. Right Away

AIDS, True Love, the Perils of Safe Sex, and Other Spiritual Concerns of the Gay Male

Gregory Flood

Brob House
"Little Books with Big Ideas"
Atlanta

First Edition 1986
Second Edition 1987

Published by Brob House Books,
P.O. Box 7829, Atlanta, GA 30309

Cover design by Pamela S. Peniston

Library of Congress Cataloging-in-Publication Data

Flood, Gregory, 1952-
I'm looking for Mr. Right, but I'll settle for Mr. Right away.

Bibliography: p. 118
1. Homosexuality, male--United States--Psychological aspects. 2. Homosexuality, Male--United States.

I. Title
HQ76.2.U5F58   1986   306.7'662   86-14718

ISBN   0-938407-00-7 (pbk.)

Printed in the United States

As I grow older and older,
And totter towards the tomb,
I find that I care less and less
Who goes to bed with whom.

--Dorothy Sayers

Dedication

To all the stars in my constellation,
especially Ken in the south,
and Pam in the west

Special Thanks

To Ken, Wayne, Joe, and Michael,
the four wise men, for all the gold,
frankincense, and myrrh

To Bobbie Reitt, for pointing out my
revealing use of the lower-case "s"

To Tom Nolan

To RS-III and the Unholy Alliance

Contents

Introduction

Wickedness is a myth invented by good
people to account for the curious
attractiveness of others.

--Oscar Wilde

There's a T-shirt on the market that says "So Many Men, So Little Sex."

Ain't it the truth?

I know that shirt is selling well because I see it on so many chests, the letters riding across the inevitably perfect pectorals (the rest of the body may look like hell, but the pecs are always porno-star perfect).

It is illuminating that so many Gay men complain about their lack of sexual fulfillment when we are purported to be the most promiscuous people on earth. Our social lives revolve around pick-up bars, and yet so many of us never manage to pick up much of anything besides.... Well, you finish that sentence for yourself.

True love is, of course, rarer than iced tea in the Sahara.

That we are scorned as sex maniacs by the bulk of society while achieving little sexual gratification in our daily lives is more irony than I care to deal with.

Why are we missing the boat?

———

Gays and Straights have one very important thing in common: we have all been taught to hate homosexuality. The fact that some of us have grown up to *be* what we were taught to despise does not exempt us from the effects of this conditioning.

I believe that we Gay men--except for the occasional rare fellow--are trudging through life under a crippling weight of lousy ideas about ourselves. I believe that these negative ideas are the causes of our lovelessness, our health crises, our financial messes, our career frustrations, and whatever other goddamnedness we find ourselves saddled with.

We are unaware of these ideas, but they are there inside us, working away. We would never consciously think such awful things about ourselves, but the *sub*conscious mind contains many surprises.

This is a book about those ideas: what they are, how we came to be functioning with them unknowingly, and, most important, how we can clean them out of our heads forever.

We will be talking a great deal in this book about the subconscious mind. It is the treasure trove of our consciousness, and the trash dump. It is from this gallimaufry of good and bad ideas, all piled on top of each other, that all our good and bad experiences arise. We will consider ways to dump the trash and keep the treasure.

We will be using the term "consciousness" a great deal. And, it seems whenever "consciousness" pops up anywhere, somebody wants a definition of it.

The definition of "consciousness" is simple: *consciousness* is a word.

What does the word mean? You already

know. So do I. So do all your friends; just ask them.

It is not my purpose to get everybody on earth to agree with the ideas in this book. I have never read a book whose every idea I could agree with, so I certainly don't expect to have written one.

Neither is it my purpose to sell you some theological bill of goods. Gay people have suffered miserable treatment at the hands of organized religion, and I understand entirely if your hackles rise at the mere mention of the word "God."

There is nothing wrong with the word "God." It is, in fact, just another word. But it is a word that, in most people's minds, is freighted with so much superstition, guilt, and anger that it is virtually unusable in our discussion here.

The purpose of this book is simply to give you some new ideas about yourself.

Maybe it already has.

Enjoy.

--Greg Flood

Part One:

Alone, in the Biblical Sense

The world has no mind of its own. The world is a reactive organism. It reacts to uncertainty with abuse. It reacts to conformity with mild contempt. It reacts to resolution with awe. And it reacts to success with great love and admiration.

--J. Kennedy Shultz

...a double-minded man is unstable in all his ways....

--James 1:8

1 Attack of the Breeders

We Gay people are raised in a society in which the religious authorities tell us we are sinners and damned to Hell, in which the psychiatrists tell us we are mentally disturbed and need to be cured, and in which the law enforcement agencies tell us we are criminals and should be locked up.

It seems we don't have much room to move.

These Gay-hating attitudes are woven into the fabric of our society, and they are drummed into each of us at an early age; words like "faggot" and "queer" are hurled as insults by prepubescent schoolboys who have no idea what the words actually mean, who know merely that a "faggot" is a very bad thing to be.

Some of those schoolboys grow up to be you and me.

———

When our Gay sex drives assert themselves at puberty, we have already been exhaustively trained to revile the very thing we find ourselves becoming.

It is a grim tribute to the power of this conditioning that closeted Gays are able, in their minds, to dance around the question of their sexual preference, always getting close without ever putting their shoe in it for years, or decades, or sometimes even their whole lives, without confessing to themselves that they are Gay.

This is the reason why "coming out," the process of admitting one's homosexuality to oneself and to others, is so terrifying for so many Gays; we are not only facing hostility from society at large, and shocked rejection by our loved ones, but we are also facing the prospect of becoming something loathsome *to ourselves.* We have accepted society's beliefs about us.

We, too, are homophobes.

———

After the confusion and emotional repression of our teen years, many of us emerge into adult life sexually obsessed and emotionally broken. Men at ages twenty-five, thirty, forty, or older find themselves going through puppy love and first rejection, emotional crises that our heterosexual schoolmates had the opportunity of experiencing in their early teens. The psychological terrors of coming out are compounded by the presence of a wife, and perhaps children, or by a homophobic career environment where homosexuality equals instant job loss. (Termination based on sexual orientation still goes on quite regularly, especially in large, intrigue-ridden corporations.)

The people who have appointed themselves the protectors of the nation's morals--every society has lots of them--point at the emotional shakiness of our lives and say, "There! You see?" as if the results of years of negative conditioning somehow proved that the basic premise behind that conditioning was valid--which is rather like burning down a house to prove it was made of ashes.

————

We are not talking here about *conscious* ideas. These negative ideas operate *sub*consciously, subtly informing our conscious thought and shaping our life experiences.

I can't believe that these profound subconscious belief systems fade away because we have sex every Friday night and get a subscription to the *Advocate.* Neither volunteer work for Gay organizations nor courageous self-pronouncements nor regular visits to the bars nor reading learned articles will unlock these dreadful mental manacles.

Spiritual problems cannot be healed by outward activity alone, not by good behavior, not by career success. If that were possible, then the psychiatrists' couches in this country would not be filled by successful people who feel that their prosperity is a fragile mask and by healthy people who cling fiercely to imaginary illnesses. Neither would the health spas and plastic surgeons' offices be crammed with people who believe that they would be loved more if they only *looked* different (a miserable notion of love), nor would there be a booming business in how-to sex manuals for couples who regard any orgasm milder than a *grand mal* seizure to be the sign of a failing relationship.

I believe that directed mental work must be done to eradicate these negative ideas in us. If nothing is done to eliminate them, then they will continue to be the foundation of our thinking and our life experiences. I believe that much of the self-deprecation, loneliness, fizzled relationships, alcoholism, drug abuse, disease, and suicide among Gays is not the product of the situational particulars of the "Gay Scene," but rather the result of an inward, subconscious conviction on our part that we are doing something perverted *just in living our lives.* This is not an idea we have asked for, but it is an idea we have accepted, however unawares, and it is an idea we must each consciously reject in order to be free of it.

———

It follows then that Gay Liberation must always be, first and foremost, an individual matter, not a political one.

This is not to say that there is no value in political activity and legislative reform. Certainly the refinement and correction of our laws is of vital importance to the well-being--indeed, to the continued existence--of the United States and should be the concern of every citizen. Those people whose talents lie in bringing about these improvements via legal action, lobbying, and political service should be given our love, our praise, our votes, and our *money*. However, we must not regard their work as being vital to our own *individual* integrity.

It would be ludicrous to propose that we will all be healthy, loved, and financially successful once a sufficient number of politicians in Washington change their minds about us. The freedom to live as we choose is ours right now as our birthright--and I'm not talking about the Declaration of Independence. This right can neither be bestowed nor rescinded by legislation. There are many examples throughout history of Gay couples' living openly as such in the midst of monstrous oppression. It is our belief in the government's authority over our individual lives that gives power to that authority. We have, in truth, always been free to live as we wished.

The quality of our lives, no matter what political environment we live in, is always determined by the beliefs and attitudes we keep alive in our subconscious minds. Negative social biases and hostile fellow citizens might influence the way we choose to express our freedom, but they cannot take it away from us. We can never be deprived of the power to control our own lives.

And that means *never.* Not by *anyone* or *anything.*

We can, however, give our power away, particularly if we don't know we have it in the first place.

Other people's attitudes about us will never change until we change our own attitudes about ourselves. We project to other people the subconscious image we have of ourselves, and this self-image is always the basis of other people's perceptions of us. To be as dreadfully feared and hated by the public as we are *must require our cooperation mentally.* Somewhere within us the oppressive opinions of Straight society must strike a responsive chord in order to do us harm.

———

For centuries the societies in which we have lived have persecuted us on the basis of our sexual orientation. In banding together for defense, we have been forced to become as obsessed with our sexual orientation as others are. We have taken on the attitudes of our detractors.

The amount of attention that Gay men give to the simple fact of their preference is *outrageous*. Know this: *Your sexual orientation is not a very important part of your psychological make-up.* It is really a rather minor, either-or consideration that has been blown up into a world issue.

It saddens me to see Gay people who want their sexual orientation to be the first thing I know about them. Their hair styles, modes of dress, bandanas, keys, gestures, and style of speaking are all geared to announcing this one thing, as if their Gayness were their most fascinating characteristic (they would have to be very dull people indeed for that to be so).

Know this also: Your sexual orientation is not a very *interesting* part of your psychological make-up, either. If someone were to ask me what I considered to be my most interesting points, my sexual preference would turn up very far down on the list, if it turned up at all.

Suppose I were to say to you, "The fact of your sexual orientation bores me. It is of no interest to anyone except you." Would you feel that I had said, *ipso facto*, that *you* were boring, that *you* were of no interest?

Gay sex is just plain old sex. It has been around as long as the human race has been around, and yet we act as if it had been discovered recently, by Oscar Wilde, or by a research team out of Cal Tech. It is an ancient and common way of life, one that really doesn't require quite so many books, learned articles, and international symposiums.

Few people nowadays would deny that physical ills can be created by mental distress. Every day it seems yet another disease--heretofore considered to be organic in nature--is added to the list of illnesses caused by psychological anguish. Migraine, ulcers, indigestion, high blood pressure, and heart attacks have been joined by bronchitis, hemorrhoids, and cancer. AIDS is inching its way into this category.

Medical science is moving toward the understanding that all physical conditions, good or bad, are the products of mental states. All disease begins with a bad idea that has been nurtured in the mind too long. Proceeding from this point is the realization that any physical ill can be healed by eliminating the ugly idea that produced it.

It would sound absurdly Victorian to call the sex urge a disease; but, if we pick that word apart, we get "dis-ease," that is, a lack of ease. And many Gay men find themselves burdened with fiercely persistent sex urges that make them profoundly dis-easy.

We somehow intuitively know that our lives depend on love. When we come to perceive our lives as loveless, we become desperately frightened, as if we were being starved to death, or dropped in the middle of a desert, or threatened with violence. Furthermore, many metaphysical practitioners around the country--Louise Hay probably being the best known--are helping people to heal themselves of supposedly incurable diseases simply by adopting a loving self-image.

The next time you find yourself getting angry with someone because he's being unpleasant to you, know this: you are becoming angry with him because *he's making it difficult for you to love him.* There is that within you that knows that if you cannot love, you will die. This unpleasant fellow is literally threatening your life.

Just so, all mental conditions produce physical manifestations. Sex is the physical outpicturing of love, and the sex urge is the physical equivalent of the spiritual yearning to love.

The need in many Gay men to find love is agonizingly intense and, to their own thinking, utterly hopeless. Just so, their sex drive is equally agonizing and equally intense because *it is the exact physical equivalent of their mental craving for love.*

That's why we sometimes feel that if we don't get some sex *we will die.* It is important that we understand what our bodies are really telling us.

When a friend says, "If I don't get laid tonight, I'll die," what he's really saying is, "I've got to get some love in my life, or I'll die."

And he's right: he *will* die.

———

Things to Consider

A. Stop making an issue of your sexual orientation. No one is as fascinated by it as you are. It is not the shining star of your personality, it is a simple, mundane personal preference that doesn't really require national television coverage (Phil Donahue notwithstanding).

I am *not* suggesting that we keep our sexuality a secret, or that we return to our closets. I'm just saying, let's not rent a billboard.

Be Gay, and enjoy your life. Refuse to allow other people to make an issue out of something that is really not very important to you. Bring your other personal qualities to the fore when dealing with anyone, Gay or Straight.

Do this: When you are dealing with Straight men, *mentally note everything you have in common with them.* Stop harping on your differences. Practice this regularly and you will be amazed at how alike in their thinking Gay men and Straight men are. The chasm separating us because of our sexual orientations is a fiction that we and they have created together.

We are all men.

B. Never use your sexual orientation as an excuse for your failures. Your relationship did not fail because there's "too much promiscuity" in Gay life. That landlord did not refuse to rent to you because he discriminates against Gays.

Your relationship failed because *you* did, and that landlord discriminated against *you*, not "Gay people." Always put the responsibility for your experiences squarely on your own shoulders, where it belongs.

C. Don't use your miserable past as an excuse for a miserable present. Your parents hurt you? Your childhood environment was oppressive? Your relationship was a disaster? I'm sorry. That stinks. I know, I've had all those problems.

But what exactly do you intend to do about all that now?

If your mother made you crazy, phooey on her. But if what she did is still pushing your buttons ten years later, who's the fool?

D. Stop being offended by other people's negative attitudes about Gays. You'll never reach a point in your life in which absolutely everybody thinks you're wonderful, so stop wasting energy in resentment.

Everyone is doing his best, no matter how dreary his "best" is. Everyone is progressing through life doing the best he knows how to do with the ideas he has to work with. *Most people who hate Gays have no personal basis for their hatred.* It is simply something they were taught to do, just as we were.

These ugly attitudes can be dealt with easily if we relate to these people out of our intellects instead of our egos. Instead of being offended by these people, get interested in them. They will appreciate it, and you.

E. Base your opinion of yourself upon your own observations.
Don't rely on other people to tell you who you are. It'll save you the trouble of getting angry when they tell you you're something you don't want to be.

Your identity is not some pre-existing package sitting around out there somewhere waiting for you to accidently happen upon it. Your identity is whatever you *decide* to be.

Set some standards for yourself.

F. Understand that your craving for sex indicates a craving for love.

AFFIRMATION

I am the creation of a perfect Intelligence that can create only that which is like Itself. It is Infinite Wisdom, Infinite Love, and Infinite Fulfillment. It expresses these qualities through me, as me.

Therefore I know that I am not a mistake. I am not here by accident. My sexual desires are implanted in me by Mind with the intention that I express them, easily and joyfully.

I am not perverted and my desires are not dirty. I am not oppressed by the negative opinions of others. I hereby reject and release any negative ideas about my sexuality, operating consciously or subconsciously, that I have been taught by others, even the negative ideas taught to me by people whom I loved very much. I am healed right now of all prejudice against myself.

My desires are clean and wholesome and correct. I embrace them, and I exercise them freely and in good conscience. I am a healthy person who was created on purpose and who is supposed to live happily.

I praise this truth and I allow it to be the foundation of my thinking and my activity now and forever.

And so it is.

2. I Left My Heart in San Francisco. And Key West. And L.A. And Fire Island. And Provincetown. And I Hear Phoenix Is Nice....

Humanity has always grooved on the idea of Fulfillment as a geographical location. The ancient world abounded in legends of advanced civilizations, always just out of sight, always located in areas that our race had not yet explored. The Greeks and Romans believed in the Hyperboreans ("Far North Dwellers") who lived near the arctic, as well as Ultima Thule ("Farthest Place"), a magical land similarly located. The Middle Ages buzzed with travelers' tales of the glorious Kingdom of Prester John, the Terrestrial Eden, and the Isle of Avalon. Millions made pilgrimages to miraculous shrines where saints dispensed divine bounty (rather like store clerks selling merchandise owned by the store). "God is not here," people were saying about their lives, "but He has a retail outlet over there." This belief, that the grace of God could be reached by boat, inspired all the Crusades.

Perhaps these legends later served to explain the savage, amoral rapacity of the European invaders of the newly discovered American continent. There, after centuries of empty legends, was a *real* undiscovered land replete with gold, jewels, haunted forests, scorching deserts, strange pagan tribesmen, bizarre animals, and magical spots like the golden city of Eldorado and the Fountain of Youth. Perhaps those centuries of legends fueled the Europeans' monstrous desire to devour this country whole, church morality--and the native inhabitants--be damned.

In recent times these legends of faraway lands became less believable as the world became better explored and satellites began to take snapshots of the globe from orbit. (One Saturday morning my friend and I were watching "Tarzan and the Lost Volcano" while we drank our coffee. My friend turned to me and said, "What kind of idiot could *lose* a volcano?")

So, we switched our belief in lost lands from "now" to "then." These perfect places used to exist, we said, but they are gone now. Thus Atlantis, and Mu, and Lemuria, all sunk, and thus the *lost* magical lore of the Egyptians, and the *lost* superscientific knowledge incinerated in the library of Alexandria.

But believing that these far countries were no longer accessible offended us on an intuitive level, so we transferred our geographical search for perfection to the next available frontier: outer space.

UFOs and Gods from Space have replaced Atlantis, and Prester John, and Ultima Thule. If there are no hidden lands on earth where happiness, wisdom, and abundance are free to all, then, we have reasoned, there must be *planets* where this is so, beautiful planets inhabited by races far older, and wiser, and more advanced than our own. (In the first Superman movie, the advanced state of life on the planet Krypton was symbolized by the absence of chairs; Kryptonians were apparently too highly evolved to sit down.)

Many popular spiritual pursuits reflect this geographical predilection. The shelves of metaphysical bookstores are crammed with books not "written by" the author, but rather "channeled through" him (it actually says that on the cover). These books allege to be the writings of superior beings, either deceased people or otherworldly, nonhuman entities, who are living in--yes, you guessed it--some other-dimensional realm where happiness, wisdom, and abundance are free to all. These entities have the knowledge we need to live well, we are told, and are sharing it with us through the medium of the person writing the book.

Also, astral projection is growing in popularity. Again, the search for truth through this technique is a geographical matter: we must free ourselves from our lumpish material bodies *(sic)* and travel off to ethereal dimensions where happiness, wisdom, and abundance are free to all.

Even Christianity, the dominant religion on this planet, tells us that we once lived in a glorious garden where all our needs were met and we spent our days in peaceful pursuits. And Christianity offers us the ultimate geographical cure: when we die we will be taken to a glittering land called Heaven where happiness, wisdom, and abundance are free to all.

It is all so familiar.

Happiness, it seems, is always somewhere else. Therefore, the conclusion becomes inescapable that all an unhappy person needs to do is to move somewhere where happiness is.

There is nothing laughable in this kind of belief. Our ancestors with their tales of enchanted lands, our contemporaries with their tales of Close Encounters and sunken continents, and all those millennia of priests who preached the glorious afterlife were all expressing, to the best of their understanding, a spiritual truth: namely, that life is *supposed* to be peaceful, and abundant, and joyful, and beautiful, and fulfilling. They intuitively knew that that was the life they should be living; and, since they were clearly not living it where they were, they reasoned that it must be available somewhere else. And so, the Isles of the Blessed, and the Holy Sepulchres, and Gods in Spaceships.

The only place they failed to look was within themselves.

This is especially curious in the case of the Christian clergy, for Jesus clearly stated, in so many words, that the Kingdom of Heaven is within you.

———

In the early 1970s, a leading Gay publication ran an article on two Gay men who had been lovers for decades. As the Gay Liberation Movement blossomed and Gay relationships began to be discussed in a positive manner, these men were frequently called upon to talk about their long-term union with various therapy groups and consciousness-raising seminars (composed mostly, I expect, of single Gay men astonished to be presented with such a durable "marriage").

The question most often asked this couple--and always in tones of anguished frustration--was, "Where did you *meet* each other?"

This question always amused the two because they had picked each other up in a public bathroom. Not real romantic. It also disturbed them, however, in that it presented them with an interesting insight: a large number of Gay men apparently thought that there was somewhere one could go where prospective lovers were more plentiful than at other places.

———

Finding a lover, it seems, or even a one-night stand, is directly related to the size of one's field of prey.

I have had many conversations with lonely Gay men who were planning on moving to some Gay mecca like San Francisco or Key

West because they thought it would be "easier to meet people there," or who were moving to some city with a smaller Gay community like Boston or Seattle because people were "less promiscuous there" (apparently from lack of opportunity).

The famous Religious Science authority Raymond Charles Barker used to answer written, anonymous questions from his audience. Once he received a note stating, "I am unhappy in New York. People are cold to me here. I have no friends. I am moving to Indianapolis."

"Good!" Barker replied to the unknown audience member. "Move to Indianapolis! Maybe somebody will like you *there* !"

The unknown writer has never stepped forward to tell us if his moving plans were changed by Dr. Barker's wonderfully blunt response, but the message to us is clear: *Love is not a location*.

How many times have we sat in groups discussing which bars we go to and why, what kind of crowd goes to which bar, and--most perplexingly--which bars it is easier to get picked up in. (I always wondered what determined that. Better lighting? *Worse* lighting?)

Now, there's nothing wrong with going out to find some good sex on a cold night. Sex is a great way to make friends, and I've seen it act as a terrific icebreaker at dull parties. However, such action must be undertaken as an exercise in the joy of living, as an expression of the fullness of your life. If sex is undertaken as a means of bolstering up your sagging self-respect, as a salve to your loneliness, or as a means of establishing your status in other people's eyes, you have some serious mental work to do.

You can't have good sex for a bad reason.

Your sexuality is no different from your money supply in that you must use it wisely if you expect it to produce good results for you. Use it poorly and, with sex as with money, you will have nothing to show for it finally but bills to be paid.

———

It is ludicrous, however, to seek love in one spot or another. You will be "Looking for Love in All the Wrong Places" until you understand that love is not some*place* and therefore *cannot be looked for at all* .

The only place you will ever find love is within yourself. If you want your life to be filled with love, then you must fill it with love on your own initiative. The Kingdom of Heaven, as they say, is within you. If you lack love in your life, then you must be brave enough to stop *looking* and start *loving*.

"Start loving who? I'm alone!"

Start loving yourself.

"I do love myself!"

Do you? Really?

I think it is instructive to examine our individual concepts of "Mr. Right." I often suspect that Gay men project their secret images of themselves into their sexual fantasies. I suspect that men who are morbidly attracted to blue-eyed, blond ballet dancers frequently fantasize *being* blue-eyed, blond ballet dancers. It is interesting that for some Gay men, the older they get, the younger their preferred sexual partners become. A man who at the age of thirty was happy with sexual partners in his own age group finds himself lusting for college students by the time he's fifty, and in his sixties he gazes longingly at photographs of sultry boys not too long out of potty training.

I believe that who we desire frequently reflects who we want to be; and when we find ourselves desiring people who have nothing in common with us, we are seeing expressed in them qualities that we feel we can never develop in ourselves. The Gays who hunger for young, young flesh I suspect see themselves as old, old, old. The ones who hanker futilely after exquisitely beautiful male models consider themselves homely, and the ones who are ashamed of their bodies always want the Scott Madsdens and the Bob Parises of the world to go home with them.

We seem to think we can excuse our faults by having a lover who doesn't share them. "It doesn't matter if I'm critical and unpleasant, because my lover is a sweetheart." "It doesn't matter if I drink to excess, and smoke, and overeat, and never exercise, because just look what I get to go to bed with every night." One begins to wonder exactly what this warmhearted, liquor-shunning Olympic gymnast is expected to see in our grouchy, sagging selves.

I believe that our concept of Mr. Right will tell us a lot about who we think we ought to be. If our Mr. Right is warm and loving, so should we be. If he is glowingly healthy and physically toned, so should we be. If he is literate and well informed, so should we be. If he is rich, so should we be.

And, if we are not any of these things, what exactly do we expect this Mr. Right to see in us when he comes along?

———

Clearly, to bring love into our lives we must stop looking for Mr. Right and start *being* Mr. Right.

Finding true love is not a matter of being in the right place at the right time. It is a matter of being the right person all the time. The place will take care of itself.

The place, in fact, will be wherever we are.

Things to Consider

A. A geographical cure will only solve a geographical problem. If you live in Oklahoma and your greatest desire is to be a scuba diver, then you have a geographical problem. If you live in Oklahoma and you feel friendless and unloved, your problem will not be ameliorated by moving to the ocean.

B. Have the courage to stop looking for love. Start living in a loving manner instead. No one else can fill your life with love. Only you can do that for yourself.

C. Know that you are Mr. Right. Examine the qualities in your fantasized Mr. Right and start cultivating those qualities in yourself. If these imaginary accomplishments are such that you have no desire to do them--i.e., if your fantasy man is a famous bodybuilder and your idea of exercise is mixing the Bloody Marys before brunch--then you need to reassess your attitude toward yourself. Your low self-esteem is causing you to desire a lover who can do all the things you can't, or won't. You want him to be--and I risk sounding like a 1940s movie poster--"everything you can never be!"

Stop focusing on your supposed inadequacies and start admiring what is good about yourself. You will soon find yourself becoming attracted to men with whom you have something in common, instead of some imaginary creature whose life can never intersect your life in any way.

D. Never respond negatively to something you want. The next time you are in a situation where someone is showing sexual interest in you, see if you can catch yourself thinking badly of him because of it. Looking down your nose at people because they desire you is not a healthy practice.

I don't know about you, but I want to be attractive. I am never rude to people who show sexual interest in me, whether or not I'm interested in them.

Always express gratitude mentally (mentally!) to someone who finds you attractive. Practice this regularly and you will become increasingly attractive to more and more people.

Affirmation

I am in the presence of Infinite Love right now. Love is the power that runs the universe and it is the power that runs me. I unite myself with it now.

I am designed to be loving and to be loved. Love is my birthright and I accept it now. I allow into my life all people who share my loving outlook, knowing that I always attract those people whose consciousness is most compatible with mine.

There is nothing in me that interferes with the action of love in my experience. I release and reject any unloving ideas or hard attitudes now operating in my consciousness.

I am a living manifestation of love, and I express that nature at all times. My life is full of love because I am filling it with love.

I praise the action of love in my mind. I am grateful for all demonstrations of love in my life, and I now release this loving power to do its good work for me now, today, and forever.

And so it is.

3. Halloween Syndrome

Given that we Gay people have come to regard love as something to be searched for some*place*, it is instructive to take a look at the places we have made for ourselves to do our searching in.

———

After the Stonewall Riots in 1969, the focus of the newly minted Gay Liberation Movement was to get us out of the bars and bathhouses and into the sunlight of day-to-day life in America. Within the space of a few years, however, that idea faded away. The bars and baths became larger, more glamorous, and more public, and Gay freedom has become a matter of being able to go to those places unmolested by police and fag-bashers.

How interesting that the dreary nocturnal lifestyle that was originally regarded as one forced on us by societal oppression is not fading out as that oppression is lifted. Rather, it is becoming more strongly established.

When a friend of mine was going over some old issues of the *Advocate* that I had around, he made a disconcerting observation: the photographs therein of the bar scene of fifteen years ago were indistinguishable from similar photographs taken only months ago. Furthermore, the photographs of bar parties in

San Francisco, L.A., New York, Atlanta, and anywhere else you care to name all looked the same: the same T-shirts, the same jeans, the same mustaches, the same keys, the same leather, the same bandanas. (A friend who heads a Gay S&M motorcycle club once wrote me out a list of what all those different colors mean, in left and right pockets. Blood-curdling.)

If our community life has changed little in the last decade, it is because we are basing it upon the same concepts about ourselves that we were using ten years ago.

Clearly, we need to develop better ideas about who we are. The Gays who stood up to the police at Stonewall were acting on a startling new idea: "We don't have to take this any more!" And, as with all great ideas, it swept the country in nothing flat. "Greater than the tread of mighty armies," said Voltaire, "is an idea whose time has come." Suddenly homosexuals all over the country were standing up to the police and saying, "We don't have to take this any more!" Organizations were organized, marches were marched, lobbying commenced, and our legal system has begun to slowly, creakingly change in our favor.

"We don't have to take this any more!" It was, is, a great idea.

It was our first great idea, and our *last*. We have, as a group, been moving forward on that idea for a long time, and I sense our momentum failing. Granted, we don't have to "take this" any more, but what exactly do we intend to "take" instead. We have asserted what we don't want, but what *do* we want? Now that we are establishing a political environment in which we feel free to live openly and as we wish, we seem to be a little at a loss as to what to do with ourselves. We have perpetuated our bar-and-bath lifestyle because we don't have any better ideas. Gay presses are forever publishing articles lamenting the empty sameness of our social lives. "Why are there no alternatives to the bars?" they cry.

The answer is obvious: there are no alternatives to the bars because not enough Gay people think highly enough of their sexuality to *produce* an alternative to the bars.

Our collective environment will never be anything more than a material equivalent of the ideas we hold about ourselves. If those ideas are ugly and self-limiting, then our environment will be ugly and self-limiting. It can be no other way.

Again--and it cannot be repeated too often--we are talking about *subconscious* thought, ingrained, long-established ideas that inform our thinking so subtly that we fail to recognize their influence.

Alternatives to the bars have been tried: one Chicago group attempted to establish weekly ice cream socials on Sunday afternoons as an alternative to nocturnal bar-hopping. The sight of all those muscle-boys in their tank-tops and mirrored sunglasses, with thumbs hooked into the loops of their sprayed-on jeans, standing around in Lincoln Park solemnly licking ice cream cones was *too funny*.

We were given an alternative environment, you see, but we came to it with the same ideas about ourselves we'd always had. Result: a Gay bar 'neath the elms without liquor. Talk about dull. Everybody finished his ice cream and went to get a drink somewhere.

A new friend once invited me to a party at his condo. He was an archaeologist associated with the local museum of natural history; very brainy, very witty. He told me it was to be an "interesting mix of people," all Gay, and that I simply *had* to be there because I had *so* much to offer.

I went to his place on the appointed night, expecting one of those terribly urban, meaningful evenings with all of us discussing art by candlelight on the terrace while drinking wines we'd never heard of before. I was delighted to have somewhere to go to socialize other than a bar.

When I got there, I discovered the place dimly lit, with blasting disco music, and all those "interesting" Gay men leaning glumly against the walls, drinks in hand, cruising.

Oh, well.

No cover charge anyway.

———

Each of us carries his consciousness around with him everywhere, and it sets about creating the same experiences for us wherever we go. It is like a good little computer that gives us back only what we've programmed into it.

This is why our problems--and our bad relationships--tend to repeat themselves, no matter what city we move to, and why all those "interesting" men at that party and all the guests at the ice cream social slipped into a cruise-bar mode of behavior automatically even though they had contrived expressly to avoid such an environment.

As children most of us were taught that God gave us free will. I interpret this now to mean that Universal Intelligence always says "yes" to our beliefs, no matter what they are. There is no Divine Stockboy up in the sky who thinks, "Greg believes in thus-and-such, but I know that will make him unhappy. I won't give it to him." Mind always gives us what we believe we will inevitably get. (Oscar Wilde, who was a better metaphysician than he knew, said, "When God wants to punish us, He answers our prayers.")

However (to refute Oscar), our negative experiences do not come to us as punishment for our shoddy thinking, they come to us simply as a *manifestation* of our shoddy thinking. "Sin" is merely wrong thinking engaged in for too long. And although we are never punished *for* our sins, we are always punished *by* them.

Life always delivers into our experience that which enables us to act out our belief systems.

The people in our lives who are causing us trouble have been brought to us by Mind in response to our beliefs about life; they are there to help us express our consciousness. We have, in effect, requested them. Like the evil genies in the Arabian Nights, they are here to fulfill our wishes, whether we like it or not.

If someone in your life is giving you a hard time, search out in your mind which of your abiding ideas about life he represents. Replace the bad idea with a good one, and he will leave you alone. You won't be any *fun* any more!

Just so, we attract our lovers through the same process. If you believe that you must sacrifice your self-respect in order to keep a lover, you will surely attract someone who will exact that price from you.

If you believe that you can have a stable relationship only by owning your lover, there are lots of very handsome young men out there who are unemployed--or who would *like* to be unemployed.

If you believe that you will never attract a lover until you are built like Jan-Michael Vincent, you will find yourself in a world full of attractive men who find you totally uninteresting sexually, and a world full of expensive health clubs offering you solace.

Do you really think you're that undesirable? Do you really think you can't attract a lover until you're so gorgeous you stop traffic? Or until you're rich as Howard Hughes? Does that seem reasonable?

If you suffer from a consistently lackluster love life, your difficulties proceed from subconscious ideas working in you without your knowledge or conscious consent. You will carry these ideas around with you everywhere, attracting the same kind of experiences, until you consciously take steps to eliminate them.

———

The gyms in my neighborhood are filled with Gay men, many of whom are trying to develop magnificent bodies while still maintaining ugly mentalities.

Most of them are still lonely. The more muscular they become, the more bewildered they seem to be. *Does anybody like me yet?* their eyes seem to say. I know some Gay men who are so self-conscious about the physiques they've developed through exercise that they can no longer walk across a room normally. (Remember the scene in *La Cage aux Folles* where Albin learns to walk like John Wayne?)

Now, there's nothing at all wrong with wanting to have a beautiful body. We must always cultivate beauty in ourselves in all ways, including our physical appearance. Our clothing and hair style should be appropriate to our self-image. If you feel your grey hair is unattractive, color it. If you've gone bald and don't like it, there are ways of fixing that. If your face sags too much, get it lifted.

Just be aware that altering your appearance will improve only the way you look. It will not make you rich, creative, loving, or loved.

Furthermore, you will still be operating from a consciousness that believes that your appearance determines the quality of your life. And, as your mind naturally continues to expand, it will begin to manifest a very natural dissatisfaction with things as they are, and you will find new physical flaws on which to lay the blame.

Trying to ease your loneliness by altering your appearance is like trying to save a burning building by redecorating the lobby. Solving your spiritual problems through material means is an endless process. Until the underlying ideas are changed, there will always be more of the problem to work on.

Before deciding how you want to look, you must first decide who you are. Then, if you still desire a change in your appearance, you will be bringing about that change for the right reason--to express who you are, not to change who you are, and not to create the impression that you are someone that you're not.

––––––––

This obsession with how we look is the product of our living situation in which pick-up bars are our principal social outlet.

The strategy engendered by these places seems to be that the more alluring we look the greater chance we have of "meeting people" (as we euphemistically refer to "getting laid"), and the more love, excitement, and satisfaction we will produce in our lives.

This is predicated on the belief that the social interaction in bars is a matter of bodies lusting after other bodies.

Know this: *the cruising in Gay bars is entirely and only a matter of consciousness seeking out compatible consciousness.* Your appearance may get people's attention, but who gravitates to you and who you meet and go home with is entirely due to your consciousness, to your deep-set, mundane ideas of what love must be for you.

If your expectations of love always include disappointment and pain, you will surely attract just the right people to affirm that for you. If you expect to achieve nothing with your cruising, you will attract no one.

That is why so many gorgeous people go home alone, or go home with people who care nothing for them as individuals. It is also why so many truly homely people seem to attract such spectacular bed partners. And, most importantly, it is why so many really pleasant, respectable-looking, intelligent, creative people go home lonely, night after boring night.

———

Many a Gay man of my acquaintance over the years has complained to me bitterly that the people he encounters are "too shallow," and that people would appreciate him more if they would only see through the surface to the "real him."

"Nobody understands who I really am!" seems to be a cry on the lips of many Gay men. Perhaps you utter this complaint yourself.

Well, you're wrong.

They *do* know the real you. They see you clear as day, frequently more clearly than you care to see yourself. That sounds very harsh, I know. Ralph Waldo Emerson put it more gracefully in his essay "Spiritual Laws":

Human character evermore publishes itself. It hates darkness--it rushes into light....If you act, you show character; if you sit still, you show it; if you sleep, you show it.

Dreadful limits are set in nature to the powers of dissimulation. Truth tyrannizes over the unwilling members of the body.

A man passes for what he is worth. Very idle is all curiosity concerning other people's estimate of us, and idle is all fear of remaining unknown.

Emerson's message to us is clear: most communication between people takes place below the surface of appearances. The most important messages we send out and receive penetrate all our disguises, all our subterfuges, and override any flattering illusions we wish to project about ourselves. (Have you ever been introduced to someone and, for no apparent reason, instantly distrusted them? Have you ever wondered how it is that Gay men can recognize each other as such at a glance?)

It may strike you as an alarming idea that anyone can see through the masks you choose to wear, but this knowledge has its comforting side: nobody can fool you either.

Unless, of course, you let them.

How many Gay men have we seen move in with some nasty, unsuitable lover, despite all our pleadings and warnings, simply because nobody else seemed to be interested in them just then? They so wanted to be able to live with someone, to have at least the appearance of a happy relationship, at least for a short while.

It is said that appearances can be deceiving. This is patently false. Appearances are deceiving only to him who wishes to be deceived, or who is already deceiving himself.

———

Things to Consider

A. If you hate the bars, don't go.

"Don't go?!"

Yeah. *Don't go.*

Stop being part of the problem. Don't worry about "meeting people." There are Gay guys all over the place just longing to get "met." (How well did you fare at the bars in that regard anyway?)

For your own mental health you must stop exposing yourself to an environment that you despise; it is spiritual suicide. You are not alone in your distaste for the bars: many Gays never go to them, or go but rarely. You will never be able to create a new social milieu for yourself until you let go of the old one.

In that same vein, never have sex with anyone you're not really attracted to, and never use drugs or alcohol out of a sense of social obligation.

In other words, enjoy the experiences you *want*, not the ones people randomly offer you.

B. There is really nothing you need to become in order to attract a relationship.

You do not need to be rich, or young, or stunningly beautiful, or tops in your field.

You need to be loving and forgiving. A person who dedicates himself to these two modes of expression can't help but attract a good relationship eventually.

As your loving consciousness asserts itself, your ideas on Mr. Right will grow and improve. Decide what you want in a lover. Set some standards for him and for yourself.

Never consider what you "need" in a lover. You need nothing. Your lover should fulfill your requirements, not make up for your limitations.

C. Develop your personal appearance so that it expresses who and what you are. Do not develop your personal appearance for the purpose of sexually exciting everyone who looks at you. It doesn't work, and it will make you a nervous wreck.

D. Never complain that nobody knows the real you.
They do!

Affirmation

I am the creation of an Infinite Mind that already has everything It wants. There is nothing I have that It needs, nor can anything I do please It or disturb Its pleasure. It is infinitely fulfilled, and It produced and maintains this universe as an expression of Its own joy.

I am an expression of that Perfect Joy and I now partake of Its fulfillment. Mind has already given me everything I require to live as I please. All I need do is accept these gifts lovingly and they will burst forth into my experience. All the wealth, creative fulfillment, physical perfection, and love that I require are granted me in every particular right now.

There is nothing in me that obstructs this flow. I hereby release and reject any ideas about my own unworthiness, or any belief that Life is displeased with me and is withholding Its good until I perform some act of penance.

There is no withholding in Mind. Its love for me is unqualified. I am the beloved of the Infinite and It bestows all of Its qualities on me right now, through me, as me, by means of my thoughts and experiences. I effortlessly attract to myself all that is best for me.

I praise the Infinite Mind that has given everything to me, I thank It for

Its unending abundance, and I accept all of
Its beautiful gifts, now and forever.
And so it is.

4. This Relationship Ain't Big Enough for Both of Us

Gay people--and people in general to be sure--routinely spend their lives in pursuit of love without ever taking a moment's thought as to what love is. (We pursue other things with a similar lack of definitions--like youth, success, and security.)

Occasionally we announce that we have "fallen in love," or we wonder if the person we are presently "seeing" (our euphemism for "having sex with") really "loves" us. The moment at which one partner says "I love you" is always a tense one: will the other say "I love you, too, Michael," or will he just say, "Thank you"? (Arrgghh!)

The desire for love is immensely powerful in us, and we intuitively sense that love is what we need to make all things well in our lives. We notice that doing things we love to do is always easier and more fulfilling than doing what we don't love, and yet we somehow never put together a definition of love for ourselves.

———

It is far easier to determine what love isn' t :

1. *Love is not nagging.* Many lovers are dreadful nags. "Comb your hair. What will people think?" "Can't you wear anything nicer

than that?" Or, my personal favorite, "You were very inattentive to me at that party!"

This is not love, it is fear of a loss of status. You are afraid that people will think less of you if you are married to a slob, or if your lover ignores you in public.

"No, no! I just want him to be the best he can be!"

You have no right to decide what somebody else's best should consist of, not even if you're married to him. Your lover is old enough to dress himself, and you are old enough to be at a party alone.

2. *Love is not putting up with someone else's vile behavior.*

"He's cruel to me, but I still love him."

Why?

It is a profound statement of your own belief in your own worthlessness that you think you must endure personal abuse in order to sustain a relationship. Clearly, you need to develop a better opinion of yourself.

Holding on tenaciously to a lover who is making you miserable is a way of admitting that you are so undesirable you fear that he will be your last lover. Or it is a stubborn refusal to admit that you made a mistake getting involved with him in the first place.

Wasting five years on a bad relationship is not a good reason to waste ten.

3. *Love is not expensive.* It is very sad to listen to some older, wealthy Gay man waxing sentimental over the deep and abiding love of his twenty-two-year-old boyfriend--for whom, by the way, he has just purchased a condo, a sports car, a Lhasa apso, and the entire Perry Ellis fall line. This is not love, it is a business arrangement. The older gentleman has purchased the rights to the younger man's ass.

There is nothing--nothing *at all* --wrong with a business arrangement. It can be a lot of fun and very rewarding to both parties involved.

Let's just not call it "love."

4. *Love is not an emotion.* Emotions are transient reactions to outward events, and the belief that love is an emotion rises from the conception of love as an influence that descends upon us from the outside, just as the phrase "falling in love" indicates the belief in the randomness of finding a mate, the Right-place-at-the-right-time school of thought that regards any meeting of true lovers to be merely a happy accident.

Love is not a reaction to accidently stumbling upon Mr. Right. *Love is a causative agent of change and growth that proceeds from within the self.* Love is not the product of a happy confluence of circumstances, it is a spiritual energy, emanating from the individual, that draws to him all that is like himself.

No one will ever come into your life and fill it with love. Only you will ever be able to do that for yourself. If there is a lack of love in your life, it is because there is a lack of love in *you*.

Many of us intuitively sense that the sterility of our personal lives is our own individual responsibility, and yet on a rational level we cannot figure out how this can be so. This produces confusion, irritation, and ultimately bitterness toward a world that seemingly refuses to cough up what we so desperately need while giving it in great abundance to other people.

———

What to do about this sorry state leads us to the question of what love is.

If I needed to answer that question only for myself, I would simply say, "Love is God." This definition satisfies me. Or I might say "Love is Growth" or "Love is Peace of Mind" or "Love is Security," because God and Love and Growth and Peace and Security are all synonymous, spiritually speaking.

That is not a definition that many people will find useful. In fact, it is an abstract definition that many of the people who read this book will not want to deal with at all.

That is fine. Nobody's saying they have to.

It will be far more instructive to deal with love in its active phase in our experience.

Consider this: *Love is what you feel toward whatever you think you can't live without.*

Given that definition, look and see what peculiar loves we have. We love jobs that exhaust us and grind us down; we wouldn't leave them for the world. We love angry, combative, and frequently violent living situations. We love poverty. And, most tellingly, we love *boredom.*

This is a far cry from our usual conception of love as that heart-fluttering rush experienced when sighting Mr. Right across a crowded room. Nor is it the usual exercise in positive thinking that tells us that if we are consistently nice to people they will be nice in return.

We are talking *spiritually* here. Certainly no adult needs to be told that if we are persistently pleasant to everyone we will receive a far higher percentage of pleasant responses. That is simple common sense, and it is kid stuff. Anybody past the age of ten knows to do this. (Whether or not they practice it is another story.)

We are talking about love as a causative agent, a spiritual power that produces and maintains the quality and the particulars of our outer experience, and that is the motive force behind any improvements we may wish to make in our lives.

This spiritual power responds to our beliefs and instantly sets about demonstrating them in our outer experience. To produce a life filled with love, we must change our beliefs *about* love.

We must let go of our destructive loves--the need for grindingly hard work, the scarcity of money, the inevitability of disease--and turn our focus onto our good loves--our inborn right to live as we wish, our natural need to be rich, our intended freedom from illness. We must give this Infinite Loving Power something new to work with in us.

———

The first thing to do is **stop thinking of love as something outside of you**, as a commodity that can be acquired.

This realization will instantly relax you, because it frees you from so much frantic *needing.* It frees you from desperate searching at the bars, from resenting people who you believe are withholding your happiness from you, from anger directed at an apparently indifferent world. You know now that what you are seeking is within you.

The next thing to do is **stop resenting happy people for being happy.** It's no crime. Never, never, never take offense at seeing qualities in other people's lives that you wish to see in your own. Don't resent lovers for being in love ("They don't look so happy to *me* !").

Don't resent rich people for being rich ("All rich people are crooks; I'm broke because I'm honest!"). Don't resent creative people for being successful ("I can do that just as well as he can, but I never got the breaks!"). And don't resent healthy, beautiful people for being attractive ("If he works on his body that much, he's either stupid or narcissistic or both!").

When you see anything you consider to be good, *praise it mentally.* Beautiful bodies, popularity, wealth, artistic fulfillment, *praise it.*

It feels good. Honest.

And that brings us to our third point:

Learn to practice forgiveness. Never try to assign blame. Proving to yourself that somebody else is causing a problem for you is not only spiritually inaccurate, it has no effect whatsoever on the problem!

Whenever someone gives you grief, instead of getting enraged, tell yourself, "I forgive this person for acting like a jerk, and I forgive myself for getting angry about it."

Simple, right?

Ha!

Forgiveness is simple for many people once they are given the technique. For me, it was like digging ditches. I was never one to give up a grudge. My thinking had to become an endless litany of forgiveness as I forgave and forgave one person after another, and always myself as well. It was a lot of work.

However, as the days and weeks passed, I found myself needing to forgive less and less. As I practiced my new attitude toward life, the Mind that *is* all life began to create a new quality of experience around me.

My life, quite simply, got better.

Try it.

Get your old dreams down off the shelf. The fantasies you entertain about how you would like to live are not fantasies at all. They are the Infinite's messages to you; they are the images of what happiness is to you.

Do you want to be rich? Then decide it is possible and start mulling over ideas of how to make it so for you.

Do you have creative longings that you've been ignoring? Get to work on one of them. It will take you places you weren't expecting to go. Nice places.

Do you wish you had a beautiful body? Well, what's stopping you? Think out a way to improve your physical appearance and set yourself lovingly to that program. (If it's painful and boring, you're doing it wrong.)

Remember, finding a lover is not a matter of being in the right place at the right time, it is a matter of being the right person all the time.

Stop looking for love and start living your life lovingly. Stop looking for Mr. Right and set about *becoming* Mr. Right.

————

Most ironically, many Gay men of my acquaintance fear that they can improve themselves *too much*, that they can become so involved with their own interests that no one will ever come along with whom they can be compatible. They are afraid of being unique.

The thinking here seems to be that your chances of hooking a husband are better if you can appeal to the widest spectrum of people possible. So, generic is good, unusual is bad.

"There aren't many men like the kind I'm looking for," they say.

Well, how many are you looking for? Most of us only want *one*. You don't have to test-drive fifty possible candidates before making a decision, you know.

Understand this: Your greatest happiness lies in what is unique about you. *Be extraordinary.* If you are truly involving yourself in all that you love, you will be surrounded by people of like consciousness, of like loves. You will never need to go prospecting at the bars again. You will find loving people everywhere that you are.

You see, the wonderful man you've been searching for is *you*. Become him, and he will stay with you forever.

You are the only person who can never leave you. Make sure you are good company for yourself.

———

Things to Consider

A. Love is what you feel toward whatever you think you can't live without.

B. What are your loves?

Affirmation

There is only one Mind, one Power, one Infinite Love operating throughout this universe. This Infinite Loving Power is operating within me right now. This Power desires nothing other than to express all of Its qualities through me, as me. This is my desire as well, so this omnipotent Mind and I are in perfect accord.

This Perfect Intelligence is the guiding force in my mind, and It always sees to it that I know what is best for me.

I do not embrace that which destroys me. I now release and reject any conditions in my experience that do not please me, whether it be financial lack, ill health, loneliness, or frustration. I have nothing further to learn from negative experiences.

The Omnipresent Mind supports me in all ways, enlightens me from within, enfolds me and protects me. It points me on my way, and I always have the good sense to heed Its advice.

I am grateful for Its good care and I joyfully release myself into It now, knowing that It has all my best interests at heart.

And so it is.

Part Two:

Deathbed Groupies

It proves what they say, give the
public what they want to see and
they'll come out for it.

--Red Skelton at the
well-attended funeral
of movie producer
Harry Cohn

The man who reads nothing at all is
better educated than the man who
reads nothing but newspapers.

--Thomas Jefferson

5. The Joy of AIDS

Everybody loves AIDS. AIDS is the greatest. We are crazy about it. We can't stop talking about it. It's on our minds every time we sit on a toilet, drink out of somebody else's glass, or kiss our mothers. It is Gay America's number-one topic for dinner table conversation; it beats the weather hands down.

The only people who don't love AIDS are the people who have it. I guess being sick makes you grouchy.

But that's okay, because we love people who have AIDS. They are our heroes. They get to go on television. Everybody turns out for the funeral.

We have discussed in earlier pages how all physical conditions proceed from subconscious belief systems. Surely there can be no doubt in our minds that AIDS is the product of an upbringing that has taught us that, as homosexuals, we have no proper place in this world. We have been convinced, subconsciously, that we have no right to live. Our bodies with their nasty sex urges have assured us a life of loneliness and alienation. End result: Our bodies cease to support us. They break down in their most crucial function: the immune system itself.

A disease that takes away your ability to fight disease is a truly perverse notion, something that a particularly wicked science fiction writer might cook up. That we have managed to inflict this upon ourselves is incredible.

Straight people are also taught to detest their sexuality, but never so fiercely as we are. So, the Straights have manifested herpes for themselves, a depressing and inconvenient condition that returns over and over. It is not, however, lethal.

The mental process by which we *unknowingly* created this illness for ourselves is the same mental process by which we can *consciously* regain our health. Life always gives us what our beliefs entitle us to. Change the belief and the experience changes equivalently. As was said by Ernest Holmes, the founder of Science of Mind, "The thing that makes you sick is the thing that makes you well."

People with Aids need, first and foremost, to change their thinking about Life and their relationship to it. *They need to realize that they have Life's permission to live.*

If that sounds simplistic--too easy to be true--don't be fooled.

An AIDS person is presented every day with powerful inducements to remain sick. His doctors--who he has been taught to believe have the last word in such matters--tell him that there is no hope. His own body produces dreadful symptoms. And, most deadly of all, he is *rewarded for being sick* by being surrounded with loving admirers. People who never gave a damn about him when he was well are suddenly falling all over him with admiration now that he is dying.

I am not accusing all these helpful people of being ghoulish. Of course, in nursing the sick, they are operating from their highest ideals of conduct. I believe that the principal reason we rally so fervently around people with AIDS is that *it feels good to be able to care for someone at last.* With Gay life as it is, filled with so much loneliness and frustration, it's a relief to finally happen upon someone who can't get along without our support.

But know this: *Helping someone to die gracefully is still just helping them to die.* Why not help them to live instead?

You *can* help them.

AIDS victims need our love, but not our sympathy. We must help them to live well, not to die poetically. It is curious to imagine "sympathetic friends" appearing on a list of the major causes of death in this country, but the day may come.

By lavishing affection on a disease victim, we are giving him this message: "We love you because you are sick." The logical extension of this idea--which the victim's subconscious will automatically make--is, "The sicker I get, the more they will love me. And if I die, there will be no end of praise for me."

Ethically, it is our responsibility to sympathize with the sick. Spiritually, however, it is our duty to refuse to accept the power of the illness; that is something we cannot do while in a sympathetic state of mind.

And, as for this disease victim needing your love, didn't he *always* need your love? Why wait until someone is on his deathbed to love him? If we were to show each other, on a daily basis, just a fraction of the love we lavish on AIDS victims, there would be no AIDS victims.

———

When I refer to denying the power of the illness, I am not suggesting physical action. Please don't go to your poor friend who is languishing with Kaposi's sarcoma, drag him out of bed, shove his running clothes against his chest, and say "All right, Randy! Enough of this AIDS nonsense! Twenty laps!"

Please don't.

Take spiritual action instead:

My friend Mark heard that his friend James in L.A. had AIDS. Mark is not an ardent metaphysician, but he has accepted the idea that all diseases begin in the mind. He determined to fly out to see James and sell him on the idea of seeing a mental practitioner.

Before he left, I told him: "Make sure James understands that your visit is not a reward to him for being sick. Make it clear to him that you are there to effect an improvement in his condition, not to hold his hand in the face of the inevitable."

Mark did just that. However, as things turned out, James could not have been less interested in spiritual healing. He came from a family of doctors and had "done time in med school," as he put it. He had a firm, abiding belief in the finality of medical knowledge.

Mark found himself in a bizarre situation. James and his "sympathetic friends" would sit around and sigh and say profound things like "We're hoping for a miracle." When Mark would suggest that James get himself to a metaphysical practitioner and get to work on his own miracle, *it was as if they could not hear what he was saying.* His words literally fell on deaf ears. His consciousness was so at odds with that of his companions that his statements failed to make any impression on their conscious minds at all.

This has not slowed Mark down one bit. Whenever he is with James, and whenever he thinks of James, he always sees him as whole, healthy, and full of energy. He has refused, in his mind, to accept the power of the disease. *Ever.*

And something very interesting has happened: James is supposed to have died by now.

He is *fine.*

He has started a new business, and it is flourishing. He has as much energy as he's ever had. He even has a "safe sex" boyfriend.

He is not suffering *any* symptoms. His life is going on pretty much the way it did before he got AIDS.

James inwardly wanted to be well, and Mark, inwardly, refused to see him as anything but. Mind has responded to the combination of James's desire and Mark's faith.

James doesn't know it yet, but he is healed.

Mark knows it. Mark never knew anything but.*

---

*Since this passage was written, James's doctors have declared him to be in remission. I think that is truly wonderful.

6. Unknown Man Has Nice Day! Details at Eleven!

The news media love AIDS better than anything. AIDS is boffo box office. For an industry that thrives on conflict and tragedy, AIDS is a Godsend. Every AIDS victim is automatically a mini-catastrophe ripe for reportage.

We are bombarded with news about AIDS from every conceivable source: TV, newspapers, magazines, movies, you name it. Science magazines report on the medical aspects, news magazines give us death tolls and projected rates of increase, and movie magazines are having a field day with poor Rock Hudson. Even sports magazines have managed to get into the act: a recent issue of a national bodybuilding periodical ran an article on how to avoid getting AIDS at the gym. (Say *what* now?)

Gay periodicals are particularly prone to this. In a recent issue of one such publication nearly every article involved AIDS in some way. Even the entertainment section told us what TV shows would be dealing with AIDS, which Broadway plays, which movies.

You'd have thought the only thing of interest Gays were doing these days was contracting lethal illnesses.

The message from the news media is simply this:

YOU AREN'T TERRIFIED ENOUGH YET!

Apparently, until we are all running through the streets screaming hysterically and tearing our hair out from fear of AIDS and throwing ourselves out of skyscraper windows in droves every lunch hour from fear of AIDS, the news media will not let up.

We need to keep in mind that these newspapers and magazines are periodicals. They must publish at regular intervals in order to survive. This means that they have a certain number of pages they must fill regularly, even when they don't have much in particular to fill them with. So, when they have nothing to *tell* us about, they must give us something to *worry* about instead.

Anxiety sells. "This new legislation might seriously effect social security benefits." It *might*?

I am not branding all journalists and their editors as fearmongers. They are bright, business-like professionals who know what their audience wants. It is not their job to decide for us what we want to read; it is their job to supply our demand, and that is exactly what they are doing.

I've always thought the idea wrong-headed that the media are responsible for educating us properly. (I am always grimly amused by parents who are outraged that television is not doing a better job of raising their children.) It is a TV news staff's job to get the highest rating possible. It is a magazine editor's job to keep his magazine in print.

It is our job, as individuals, to listen to the ideas presented by the media and to accept them or reject them intelligently and as we please.

A recent edition of a national Gay publication had a center-page spread of news bits about AIDS from around the country. Each paragraph was headed with the name of its city of origin, and the short news item would follow. In the bottom right-hand corner, in a tiny box, was a miniscule mention of a man named William Calderon, who had allegedly used mental techniques to bring about his complete recovery from AIDS.

Surely Mr. Calderon's wonderful achievement should have been front-page news. But the necessities of survival in periodical publishing had to come first: the cure for AIDS will only be one story. The continued advance of the disease makes for a thousand stories. (About the same time, *New Realities* magazine ran an extensive cover article on Calderon. It is very interesting reading.)

The mental program that Calderon engaged in is a blueprint for anyone seeking to bring about a metaphysical healing for an illness. One such program is outlined at the end of this section..

Until recently, the various AIDS support groups did little to engender a healing consciousness in their members. The well-intentioned volunteers shared the same sense of hopelessness as the disease victims.

"Meetings" involved little more than glum pronouncements of the spread of the disease and other statistics. Apparently, it was believed that the victims would feel better if they could be assured that many other people were dying right along with them.

However, and contrary to common belief, misery doesn't love company.

Given that AIDS is the product of negative mental patterns, the practice of herding its victims together into a room at regular intervals to impress them with the growing destructive power of the illness is the most disastrous course of action possible.

But the situation is changing.

People, it seems, are not dying on schedule. Many Gays are successfully utilizing mental techniques to heal themselves, either by following Calderon's lead, or through intuitive discoveries of their own methods, or by becoming involved with one of the many New Thought ministries.

The AIDS support groups, to their credit, are growing very curious indeed about all this. Some of them have begun metaphysical healing programs.

High time!

———

The various systems of metaphysical healing are not in competition with the medical sciences. Most practitioners of these systems simply want people to be healed. Not "Healed my way," but just healed, period. They are believers in whatever truly works.

When a doctor tells you a disease is incurable, he is simply saying that he knows no method of helping you. No doctor really thinks that AIDS or any disease is literally incurable; otherwise, no cure would be sought. Never accept a doctor's diagnosis as a death sentence. He didn't give you your life and he can't take it away from you. He's just saying that he can't help you. Don't go to your grave because he said you're supposed to.

There is really no reason to be *that* polite to your physician.

———

7. Safe Sex: Robbing Your Peter to Pay Paul

Your immune system, like all of your body and its desires, is a physical outpicturing of spiritual laws. Your immune system is a material representation of your divine right to live in harmony with the world. It is the monitoring system that sees to it that you are unmolested by the microorganisms that come your way. It is spiritual Harmony in action. When this system breaks down, it indicates a fundamental breakdown of good ideas. A belief has been embraced in the victim's mind, a belief that the world is inimical to him, that he has no proper place in it.

To undo this mental mess requires rethinking one's concepts of life on all levels. Just because AIDS is transmitted sexually does not mean that its implications in the mind are exclusively sexual also. *AIDS is not a homosexual disease.* It is a disease engendered in a singled-out sociological group whose members have mutually accepted an array of lousy ideas about themselves. Think of any put-upon minority and you will realize that each has some awful disease unique to it.

Many of us are trying to angle our way around this spiritual law by engaging in "safe sex" techniques. The reasoning here is that one can't acquire AIDS if the proper conditions for contagion are avoided.

That's true as far as it goes. Realize, however, that the negative subconscious patterns that produce AIDS in others may still be operating in you, and the law of Mind dictates that all beliefs must manifest eventually. You may avoid getting AIDS by having only "safe sex," but those ugly mental patterns must surely manifest something equally dreadful for you at last, either in your body or in your outer experience.

Furthermore, when we engage in a particular form of sex for the express purpose of avoiding something we fear, we are graphically and powerfully reinforcing whatever ideas are producing the fear.

We cannot escape responsibility for our thinking by carefully controlling our outer activity. As we are told in the Book of Job, that which we fear will come upon us, in one form or another, inevitably.

The only sex that is safe is that which is engaged in for good reasons, with a loving consciousness and a clear belief in the rightness of it.

The only life that is worth living is that which is engaged in for good reasons, with a loving consciousness and a clear belief in the rightness of it.

The only reason that reality is out there at all is to let us see what is going on in our consciousness. If we wonder what our belief systems are, we need only look at our outer experience. It is a mirror that reflects our consciousness back at us.

AIDS has come with a message, and that message is this:

"It is time to stop thinking ill of yourself. It is time to take your right and timely place in this world. You have Life's permission to live, or to die. It is time for you to choose."

To heal your life, you must heal your thinking.

Some people would rather die than change their minds.

Are you one of them?

———

If You Are Diagnosed as Having AIDS

1. Decide to live.

2. Refuse to associate with people who believe in the inevitable consequences of your condition. (No deathbed groupies!) Deal only with people who joyfully support your belief in your own ability to heal yourself. *This includes your doctor.* Find one who is at least intrigued by your intended course of action.

3. Refuse to accommodate the disease. Live your life normally. Go to work, and to play, as always. (This does not include having sex with people to whom you could transmit your condition.)

4. Practice forgiveness--of everybody, all the time. This will enable you to free yourself from your past. It is your reservoir of negative ideas, after all, that is creating the damage.

5. Get involved in some organized program that praises you for what you are, rather than condemning you for what you've done, and that teaches you that you can change anything about yourself that you choose. (Calderon did est. Good. Since I am involved with Religious Science, I, of course, recommend it highly, along with Unity, and the many independent New Thought ministries.)

6. Engage in a regular program of creative visualization and positive mental treatments. There are many good books on this technique, and any metaphysical practitioner worth a nickel can help you learn it.

7. Follow all this up by engaging in whatever activities you believe are in line with your healing. You might want to consult a nutritionist or take up an exercise program or learn to play a musical instrument. Whatever your own good sense recommends to you.

Affirmation

There is only one thing in the universe, and that is Mind. Everything proceeds from Intelligence and is made of It. Everything in the universe is an expression of Its perfect orderliness.

That means I am an expresssion of that perfect order. The perfect wholeness of the Infinite is the pattern of my body and I will have it no other way. Every cell, organ, and function of my body has at its center a core of Perfection and Harmony that maintains it in perfect operation.

There are no negative ideas active in my consciousness now that could produce any kind of negative physical experience for me.

I declare now that my body is being washed clean, within and without, by a fountain of Divine Purity that cleanses me of any stain or blemish.

I accepts Life's plan for me. I allow my physical perfection to be so now. I love this body I am living in and I move about in it easily and freely.

I thank Infinite Mind for this happy completeness of form It has given me, and I realease this treatment now, knowing that it is the truth about me, now and forever.

And so it is.

Part Three:

The Fag-Basher in the Sky

The Puritans hated bear-baiting, not because it gave pain to the bear, but because it gave pleasure to the spectators.

---Thomas Babington Macaulay

Many a long dispute between divines may be thus abridged: It is so. It is not so. It it so. It is not so.

--Benjamin Franklin

8. If God Is the Answer, I Want a Second Opinion

When I was coming out of my closet (back before the comet killed the dinosaurs), the budding Gay Liberation Movement coined the phrase "Gay is Good." It sounded nice, but I almost immediately responded with, "Good for What?"

After all, as Henry David Thoreau said, "Don't just be good. Be good for something."

Certainly I could see that in a free society all people should be free. I could see that homosexual activity did no harm and did not deserve persecution. But that was merely to say "Gay is Okay," "Gay is socially acceptable."

But *Good?*

––––––

I was a deeply religious kid, and the conflict between my moral attitudes and my sexual desires ultimately resolved itself into a conflict between my religious beliefs and my common sense, and that I ultimately came to perceive as a conflict between my *church-given* religion and my *God-given* intelligence.

I soon found it impossible to believe in most people's God, that cranky old man with the long, white beard sitting on a throne in outer space, looking down over the world (which He supposedly created) shaking his head gravely and saying, "Oh, this will never do!"

This God was an incompetent builder who could not get Creation right the first time. He had to keep wiping the slate clean and starting over, once by casting Adam and Eve out of Eden, then by flood, then by the sacrifice of His own son, and again--soon--by fire.

This God had given me desires that He regarded as disgusting and had then sadistically forbidden me to express them, cursing me with disease when I did. This God was all-loving, except for people like me, of whom He thoroughly disapproved; all-merciful, except toward people like me, whom He threatened with eternal damnation; and all-wise, except for His curious tendency to create things that He didn't like (Satan, and war, and faggots).

This God had created a system of living that worked like this: We are born into the world and make our way, often without any moral guidance whatsoever, and stumble along through loneliness, illness, frustration, and financial lack. When we seek a means of anchoring ourselves, we are confronted with a multitude of religions all claiming to be the Only True Faith. We grow older, and sicker, and dimmer, and more helpless, and more useless, wondering all the while what the purpose of it all is, our bodies deteriorating more and more with each passing year, until we finally die, to pass on to our final reward, provided that our past conduct can stand up under the judgment of this self-same implacable Deity whose moral laws *have never been coherently explained to us in the first place.*

Well, I thought, that's enough of that. A second-grader could have devised a fairer system.

Whatever the Creator was, He--It--was something far more complex, subtler, and more loving than this irritable, legalistic, fag-bashing absentee landlord in the sky who had dominated my thinking for decades.

Over the years my concept of God evolved. I began to perceive what appeared to be an Intelligence operating in all things and through all things, an all-pervasive Presence that did not seem judgmental or frightening at all. I began to suspect that God was on the side of "His" creations after all.

I eventually developed a concept of an intangible, nonanthropomorphic God. And then I encountered people who had beaten me to the punch long ago, people like the Religious Scientists and their very distant cousins the Christian Scientists, and the Universalists, the Unitarians, the Quakers, the Transcendentalists, the Deists, the Platonists, people like Ernest Holmes, Thomas Troward, Ralph Waldo Emerson, Benjamin Franklin, Thomas Jefferson, Immanuel Kant, Brother Lawrence, Plotinus, Plato, and, most astonishingly, a much-misunderstood Jewish rabbi called Jesus.

One day, I made this realization:

Any telescope would afford me a view of thousands of galaxies. And in each of those galaxies were trillions of stars. And around those stars orbited quintillions of planets. And on one of those planets, in an insignificant quarter of a humdrum sort of galaxy, was a speck of a creature named Greg Flood who believed that whom he had sex with on Saturday nights could cause anguish in the colossal Intelligence that had created all that universe.

That, I realized, was a really gigantic kind of egotism.

People have been put in padded cells for less.

———

I believe that "Loving" is simply a matter of perceiving this intangible God within every part of Its creation. The great Christian divine Brother Lawrence called this "Practicing the Presence." To deliberately view each person as a perfect expression of a Perfect Mind, operating in life to the best of its ability, saves you a world of arguing. To see the core of Perfection and Wholeness tucked inside each one of us is a tremendous healing exercise.

Mothers are famous for this ability. We will be watching a newscast about some sick man who has, say, raped a busload of nuns and then set them on fire. The killer's tearful mother will then appear on the screen with a mike stuck in her face and cry, "He's really a *good boy* down deep!"

Yeah, lady, *way* deep.

But of course she is absolutely right. Within the very worst of us is a spirit of purity and strength that is never depleted or soiled by our stupidities. A mother's insistence that her wayward child is really a "good boy" is not a refusal to face reality. It is, on the contrary, a keen awareness of reality, of the Truth below the appearances.

Most of us talk about "liking" and "loving" as if they were different intensities of the same feeling. "We like each other now, and it may grow into love."

I think our new definition of love refutes this.

"Liking" simply means that you find certain people agreeable. Their looks, behavior, interests, and attitudes strike enough of a responsive chord in you that you enjoy their company.

"Loving" is something very different. Loving is the practice of seeing through these surface realities of person and attitude to view the untouched Being within.

It is easy to *love* people you don't *like.* One has nothing to do with the other. After all, Jesus said, "Love your enemies." He didn't say, "Make everybody your friend." His statement clearly allows that we will *have* enemies. He simply said to love them anyway.

And so we discover that "Love" and "Forgiveness" are the same thing.

When you are in a negative confrontation with someone, take a step backward mentally and try to see the perfect Spirit operating at the center of this stupid jerk you're fighting with. It does wonders for your blood pressure. Practice this loving technique diligently and you will find yourself *liking* more and more people.

And don't forget to include yourself. Always feel free to look through your own surface appearances to the quiet Wholeness at your center. From that vantage point you can painlessly evaluate your virtues, and your nonsense.

———

9. Beggars in Heaven

Whole forests are being chopped down and turned into paper in order to print books about Gays and the Bible. This is a hot issue nowadays. Well-meaning exegetes are popping up everywhere explaining how this or that passage in Paul or Leviticus wasn't *really* anti-Gay, or how it was merely reflecting a hygienic, reproductive imperative of the times.

Such a waste of good trees.

Let's face it: Many of the authors of the Bible *despised* homosexuals and said so. If you are a person who believes that God wrote the Bible, then you must believe that God despises homosexuals as well. Period. No getting around it.

It is interesting--and significant--that Jesus had nothing whatever to say on the subject. He never mentioned it. The bulk of these anti-Gay passages appear in the writings of Paul of Tarsus.

"Saint" Paul.

Paul--who never met Jesus--disapproved of sex in general, even between husband and wife, and was desperately trying to establish some kind of regularity in the sex lives of converts who had come to Christianity out of pagan religions that permitted all kinds of sex and that practiced ritual orgies as a part of worship, even to the point of maintaining sacred prostitutes in some temples.

When Paul was giving advice on conduct and morality, he was pedantic, biased, oppressive, and very boring. When he described the workings of the Soul, however, he soared above his dreary personal prejudices.

He was a great metaphysician.

In his highly successful campaign to organize and unite the early Christians into a structured church, Paul embraced a rather self-serving theology that carried Jesus's message but wrapped it up in the vocabularies of the old religions so as to attract converts from those faiths. As a result, many of Paul's finer spiritual writings have been grossly misinterpreted by later Christians, producing "Christian" religions whose tenets bear very little resemblance to the teachings of the gentlemen carpenter from Nazareth.

When Paul wrote his famous epistles, he was writing to people he had taught himself or who had been taught by his representatives. So, he used terminology and made references that he knew his followers would understand perfectly without explanation; he did not attach a glossary to his letters so that all those future generations of scholars would understand what he meant. If Paul had known that exegetes would be pouring over his little corporate memos for centuries after his death and regarding their every comma and semicolon as the Word of God, I'm sure he would have been much more careful about what he said.

We Gay people have come to regard Paul as our enemy. I think that is a terrible mistake. Certainly Paul disapproved of homosexuals-- loudly, in fact.

But then, he disapproved of so many things.

————

If we read Paul's epistles with an open mind, we see that he used the terms "Jesus," "Christ," and "Christ Jesus" as describing *three different things.*

"Jesus" was a person.

"Christ" was the Divine Mind operating through each individual.

"Christ Jesus" was a way of saying that the Infinite Mind, the Christ, operated with full authority in the consciousness of Jesus. It was used to describe both the man and his teaching.

Given this explanation, listen to what Paul is telling us in his letter to the churches in Galatia:

Now, before faith came we were confined under the [Mosaic] law, kept under restraint until faith should be revealed. So that the law was our custodian until Christ came, that we might be justified by faith. But now that faith has come, we are no longer under a custodian; for in Christ Jesus you are all sons of God:...There is neither Jew nor Greek, there is neither slave nor free, there is neither male nor female; for you are all one in Christ....

-Gal. 3:23-28

Christ, the Infinite Mind, God (if you please), is within each of us. Paul is telling us that Infinite Mind is no respecter of persons. Divine Intelligence works through all people with equal power, regardless of the particulars of their lives and bodies. No one--no, not even a Gay person--is a pauper pleading for mercy from a disapproving God. We are each an outlet of Divine Power, able to stand eye-to-eye with any other member of our race.

Gay is good because people are good. Gay is good because you are good and I am good.

In Heaven, within us, in Spirit, there are no men or women, no Gays or Straights.

And there are no beggars either.

———

Postscript

There goes the good time that was had by all.

--Bette Davis
remarking on a
passing starlet

The purpose of this book has been to give you some new ideas about yourself. I know it has been successful in this, because it has given me new ideas about myself in the writing of it.

If this book has a message, it is simply that you are unlimited. It is your purpose in this life to establish an intelligent working relationship with Life itself. You have within you a perfect power that will give you everything you require if you will just take the time to get your thinking tidied up. This power is unimpressed by your past successes, and it is unimpeded by your past mistakes, your upbringing, or your present environment. It is not impressed by AIDS. And It certainly makes no bones about your sexual orientation.

There will be no mass conversions to the ideas in this book. This concept of Divine Mind has been active in this country since before we were called the United States, and scientific spiritual healing has been going on regularly, and with tremendous success, for 150 years, and yet these things are utterly unknown to most Americans, and are regarded as quackery by most doctors.

As Mark discovered with James's "sympathetic friends," these ideas can stimulate only a consciousness that is ready for them.

The healing of the Gay lifestyle must proceed from each individual living in it, not from some group "ah-*ha!*"

We have all heard the hymn "Let There Be Peace on Earth, and Let It Begin with Me." Putting that to our own purposes, we say, "Let There Be Gay Freedom, and Let Me Begin by Freeing Myself."

We cannot change all Gay society. We cannot change the way other people behave at all. But we can, as individuals, refuse to go on being part of the problem--at all, any more, *right now.*

I have scrupulously avoided suggesting any "alternatives to the bars" and such like. Any attempt to do that becomes as divisive and silly as that awful ice cream social. Until we change our underlying beliefs about ourselves, almost any gathering of Gay men, convened for whatever purpose, will turn into an impromptu bar scene because that is all we are able to demonstrate out of the ideas we've got.

Any newer, cleaner, more open Gay lifestyle will arise organically from us once enough of us have accepted newer, cleaner, more open ideas about what we are. We can never successfully impose these changes upon ourselves from the outside.

It is time for us Gay people to tidy up our thinking. We have struggled long enough with other people's ugly opinions of us. It is time for us, as individuals, to face what has been randomly implanted in our minds, and to change our minds to suit ourselves.

We no longer have any time for mental delaying tactics. With the advent of AIDS, our clocks have begun to tick. We must grow, or die. This is not an ultimatum. It is simply a choice we must now make.

Some people will choose to die. That is all right. They will consider the ideas in this book to be a little too strange, too spooky, too far-out to deal with.

That is entirely their choice to make. Personally, I intend to live on to a very strange, spooky, far-out old age.

I invite all of you--each of you--to make the journey with me.

END

Envoi

Many shall come in the name of Truth and say, do this, or do that--music, dancing, all sorts of amusements. But Truth says beware, be not deceived, seek first the truth, and all the above will be a pleasure to you.

This is a trying scene to go through; it seems as though you must leave all the world's pleasure, and seclude yourself from society. But this is not the case; you will like society all the better.

--Phineas Parkhurst Quimby
(1802-1866), originator of
Scientific Spiritual
Healing in America

Appendix: Further Reading and Listening

The books are available in the self-help sections of most mainstream bookstores. The cassettes may be a little tougher to locate; check your local metaphysical bookstore, or contact the nearest Religious Science Church or Unity Church. Louise Hay's books and tapes are also available through Hay House in L.A. Ken Shultz's tapes are available only from the Atlanta Church of Religious Science, Suite 312, 455 E. Paces Ferry Rd. NE, Atlanta GA 30305.

New Thought: General and Introductory

Frederick Bailes, Hidden Power for Human Problems

Raymond Charles Barker, Collected Essays
The Science of Successful Living

Emmet Fox, The Mental Equivalent

Shakti Gawain, Creative Visualization

Thaddeas Golas, A Lazy Man's Guide to Enlightenment

Louise L. Hay, You Can Heal Your Life

Ernest Holmes, This Thing Called You

Gerald Jampolsky, Love is Letting Go of Fear

William Parker, Prayer Therapy

J. Kennedy Shultz, (Cassette Albums)
Basic Principles of the Science of Mind
Applying the Principles of the Science of Mind
The Practice of Spiritual Mind Treatment

New Thought: AIDS and Sexuality

Louise L. Hay,   AIDS: A Positive Approach (cassette)
Doors Opening: A Positive Approach to Aids (Video)

J. Kennedy Shultz,   Shultz on Sex & Spirituality (Cassette Album)

Betty Clare Moffat,   When Someone You Love Has AIDS